JOURNAL

LEGACY

JoAnn S. Dean

All rights reserved. No part of this product may be reproduced, scanned, or distributed in any printed or electronic form without permission.

"Nothing will steal your strength like living a life you do not understand or love."

This journal is a companion for the book Self-Care for Success.™

In Self-Care For Success, JoAnn empowers the reader to pause for the purpose of Reconnecting with who they are, Reassessing what they value and Rising to live out and leave a legacy.

It is in our understanding of who we are, we can heal and break behavior patterns, building a stronger foundation for our families. When we don't know who we are, it shows up in our decision making. It's time to take responsibility for our lives and the roles we play in the lives of others. We are all here to live and love, grow, and glow, and to serve and shine our light. Our lives and legacies matter, someone is depending on us.

Available @www.joanndean.com

Legacy Builder

I feel the rhythm in my walk, the cadence in my talk.
The shifts, the call and its rewards.

A new day has dawned asking me to carry on.
Seasons are sacred, they highlight my hidden spaces.

Spring, Summer, Winter & Fall they all seem to demand a different call.

The winters warn me spring is coming, prepare your strategy to tell your story, because it will illuminate the path for God's glory.

Fall into hiding, reflect and refuel. The summer months will require all of you.

Strategy is key, it's how you live free.
Don't hold back, allow yourself to be.

Spiritual insight has taken flight, recognize your connect is getting you all the way right.

JoAnn Dean

Legacy Love Letter

DATE ————————————

_____
_____
_____
_____
_____
_____
_____
_____
_____
_____
_____
_____
_____
                                    _____

This journal belong to

_____

Born _____

Location _____

Parents
_____
_____

Grand Parents
_____
_____
_____
_____

Great-grand Parents
_____
_____
_____
_____

Cherished Children

"Understanding who you are is the foundation for a successful life."

~ JoAnn Dean

What do you consider your motto?

_____
_____
_____
_____

What is some of the best advice you've received?

_____
_____
_____
_____

What do you value?

_____
_____
_____
_____
_____
_____
_____
_____

5 minute message

What I want you to know

_____
_____
_____
_____
_____
_____
_____
_____
_____
_____
_____
_____
_____
_____
_____

Sibling Names & Birthdays

Family Traditions

Memories of Parents

5 minute message

What I want you to know......

"My mission in life is not merely to survive, but to thrive; and to do so with some passion, some compassion, some humor, and some style."

~Maya Angelou

What do you do for a career?

_____
_____
_____
_____

What are your greatest strengths?

_____
_____
_____
_____

What makes you stop and go WOW?

_____
_____
_____
_____

5 minute message

What I want you to know.....

Ideas & Inspiration

What scares me?

_____
_____
_____
_____
_____
_____
_____

How I move through the fear?

_____
_____
_____
_____
_____
_____
_____
_____

Share a Life Lesson

5 minute message

What I want you to know......

5 minute message

What I want you to know......

5 minute message

What I want you to know......

5 minute message

What I want you to know......

5 minute message

What I want you to know......

Accomplishments

5 minute message

What I want you to know......

5 minute message

What I want you to know......

My favorite color
_____

My favorite song
_____

My favorite time of day
_____

My favorite snack
_____

My favorite book
_____

*"If you get, give.
If you learn, teach."*

~Maya Angelou

5 minute message

What I want you to know......

5 minute message

What I want you to know......

5 minute message

What I want you to know......

5 minute message

What I want you to know......

5 minute message

What I want you to know......

Reflecting on Relatives.......

5 minute message

What I want you to know......

_____
_____
_____
_____
_____
_____
_____
_____
_____
_____
_____
_____
_____
_____
_____
_____
_____
_____
_____
_____
_____

5 minute message

What I want you to know......

5 minute message

What I want you to know......

5 minute message

What I want you to know......

5 minute message

What I want you to know......

_____
_____
_____
_____
_____
_____
_____
_____
_____
_____
_____
_____
_____
_____
_____
_____
_____

"Success is liking yourself, liking what you do, and liking how you do it."

~Maya Angelou

5 minute message

What I want you to know......

5 minute message

What I want you to know......

5 minute message

What I want you to know......

5 minute message

What I want you to know......

5 minute message

What I want you to know......

"There is no greater agony than bearing an untold story inside you."

~Maya Angelou

5 minute message

What I want you to know......

5 minute message

What I want you to know......

5 minute message

What I want you to know......

5 minute message

What I want you to know......

5 minute message

What I want you to know......

What vision do you have for your family?

5 minute message

What I want you to know......

5 minute message

What I want you to know......

Do you have an unfulfilled dream?

5 minute message

What I want you to know......

5 minute message

What I want you to know......

5 minute message

What I want you to know......

5 minute message

What I want you to know......

5 minute message

What I want you to know......

Fondest Memory

5 minute message

What I want you to know......

5 minute message

What I want you to know......

5 minute message

What I want you to know......

5 minute message

What I want you to know......

5 minute message

What I want you to know......

A message to my grandchildren

5 minute message

What I want you to know......

5 minute message

What I want you to know......

5 minute message

What I want you to know......

5 minute message

What I want you to know......

5 minute message

What I want you to know......

"If you don't like something, change it. If you can't change it, change your attitude. Don't complain."

~Maya Angelou

Do you have any mentors?

5 minute message

What I want you to know......

5 minute message
What I want you to know......

5 minute message

What I want you to know......

5 minute message

What I want you to know......

5 minute message

What I want you to know......

"You can only become truly accomplished at something you love. Don't make money your goal. Instead pursue the things you love doing and then do them so well that people can't take their eyes off of you."

~Maya Angelou

5 minute message

What I want you to know......

"Carve your name on hearts, not tombstones. A legacy is etched into the minds of others and the stories they share about you."

~ Shannon Adler

5 minute message

What I want you to know......

5 minute message

What I want you to know......

5 minute message

What I want you to know......

5 minute message

What I want you to know......

Aligned & Divine

To be aligned is divine, otherwise it's a misuse of our time.

Purpose driven, pushed by passion, your souls blueprint is everlasting.

Each assignment mapped out precisely, you're the co-creator building the dream, learning the lessons and experiencing each scene.

Platforms, Skyscrapers, Monumental museums, they're the entryways for brighter days, our children need. Leveraging the game of life to ensure they take part in its delight. With heads held high and trumpets blaring to the sky they understand the mission, it's time to switch positions.

A spiritual team sits high delicately directing from the sky. They cheer you on and hold up your arms, you got this they say, we're with you all the way.

Remain on course, believe you're a force. Here to serve humanity and sideline some of this life's insanity.

Born to boldly BE you, blessed, impressed doing your best, is the highest compliment of all. It leaves your creator smiling and standing tall. So go ahead answer the call, independently embrace all of who you are.

~JoAnn Dean

Do you have any mentors?

5 minute message

What I want you to know......

5 minute message

What I want you to know......

5 minute message

What I want you to know......

5 minute message

What I want you to know......

5 minute message

What I want you to know......

"I've learned that people will forget what you said, people will forget what you did, but people will never forget how you made them feel."

~Maya Angelou

I'm grateful for....

5 minute message

What I want you to know......

5 minute message

What I want you to know......

How my faith impacted my life......

Personal Message

About the Writer

JoAnn Dean has been helping others gain clarity, elevate their confidence, and move into action for over 20 years!

She's known for being a trustworthy thought leader with a calm demeanor who over delivers. She privately empowers professional women to lead purposeful lives by focusing on the value of self-care, investing in, and putting themselves first. This leads to growing in areas they didn't anticipate, recapturing their power and decoding programming that no longer serves them.

JoAnn is the Founder of Inspired By JoAnn, LLC, a community created for the professional woman to pause from pouring into others, reconnect with herself, heal and embrace who she is through the support of Personal Life Coaching, Messages of Inspiration & The Exclusive Self-Care For Success Circle Membership Community.

She is a seven-time self-published author. She's a graduate of Southern University at New Orleans, where she obtained both a Bachelors & Master's Degree in Social Work. She is Board Certified Personal Life Coach. She is an alumnus of DeVos Urban Leadership Initiative and Life Purpose Institute where she obtained her Life Coaching Certification. JoAnn was featured in VoyageATL Magazine in 2019.

Her mantra: I give thanks for a perfect day. God is my unfailing supply. Miracles and signs follow me and wonders never cease. Divine love floods my consciousness. My mind is brilliant. My body is healthy. My spirit is tranquil. All is well. I am complete. And it is so.

Her mission is to create a community of 100 women with the focus of self-care, sisterhood, and spiritual growth.

Follow | @selfcare_for_success
www.joanndean.com

"The need to leave a legacy is our spiritual need to have a sense of meaning, purpose, personal congruence, and contribution."

~Stephen Covey

Inspired By JoAnn
"COACHING YOU TO CLARITY"

Thank You!